A First Look
GOD

Lois Rock

Illustrated by Carolyn Cox

Educational consultant: Margaret Dean

A LION BOOK

Bible passages mentioned in this book:

1   Psalm 24, verses 1 and 2.
2   Psalm 104, verses 10 to 12, and 18.
3   Psalm 65, verses 9 to 11.
4   Psalm 100.
5   Genesis, chapters 7 to 9; also Psalm 7, verses 10 and 11.
6   Psalm 119, especially verses 4 and 105.
7   Luke, chapter 15, verses 11 to 32.
8   Psalm 131.
9   Matthew, chapter 12, verse 50.
10 Psalm 23.
11 Psalm 68, verses 7 to 10, and 20.
12 Psalm 25, verses 11 to 14.
13 2 Corinthians, chapter 3, verse 18; also 2 Timothy, chapter 1, verse 7.

Text by Lois Rock
Copyright © 1994 Lion Publishing
Illustrations copyright © 1994 Carolyn Cox

The author asserts the moral right
to be identified as the author of this work

Published by
Lion Publishing
850 North Grove Avenue, Elgin, Illinois 60120, USA
ISBN 0 7459 2496 4

First edition 1994
10 9 8 7 6 5 4 3 2 1

Library of Congress Cataloging-in-Publication Data
Rock, Lois, 1953—
        A first look at God / Lois Rock
        ISBN 0–7459–2496–4
    1. God—Juvenile literature. [1. God.] I. Title.
    BT107.R63   1994
    231–dc20   94–9715 CIP

Printed and bound in Singapore

Contents

Introduction
Who is
God?

Who is God?
And why do people talk about him?
You can't see anyone called God!
So what *can* people know about him?
Does he exist at all?

Christians believe there is a God.
They read about him in their special book,
the Bible, which includes writings that Jews
read and stories that Muslims know.

In the Bible, Christians read about the things God has done, the things he has said.
They discover more about the God—

● who made the world, and looks after it

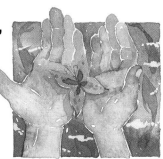

● who loves good and hates evil

● who cares for people, and wants them to be his friends

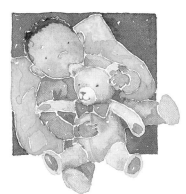

● who is more powerful than anything in the world, even though no one can see him.

In this book, you can discover some of the things the Bible says about God.

1 Let's look at
The sky

Have you seen the sky?
The golden sun high above you
the shimmering blueness
reaching down to the far horizon ...
drifting clouds, silver, white and grey ...
the sliver of a crescent moon slicing through the blackness of night ...
the glittering stars ...
the whole universe.
Have you ever wondered how it came to be the way it is?
Or why it exists at all?

Throughout the ages, many people have believed that the world exists because God made it.
That is what Christians today believe.
This is a song from the Bible, written hundreds of years ago, by people who believed in God:

The whole world
and everything in it
belongs to God
who made it.

From Psalm 24 of the Bible

God is the maker of the world.

2 Let's look at
Living things

Think of all the plants and animals
in the world...
in mountains
deserts,
meadows,
forests,
seas,
cities...
everywhere!

Thousands of years ago, the people who
lived in a country called Israel looked with
amazement at the wonderful world around
them. They believed that God had made it all.

Today, Christians still sing the song the
Israelites sang to him long ago:

You make springs flow in the valleys,
and rivers run between the hills.
They provide water for the wild animals;
there the wild donkeys drink the water they need.
In the trees nearby
the birds make their nests and sing.
The wild goats live in the high mountains,
and wild hyraxes hide in the cliffs.

From Psalm 104 of the Bible

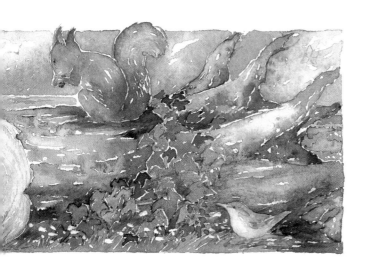

God is the giver of life.

3 Let's look at
Our food

The sun shines,
the rain falls,
to make plants grow.
There is so much to harvest...
leaves,
stems,
roots,
fruits,
seeds...
food for
people
and animals.

Long ago, the farmers in Israel thanked God for making a world that produced good harvests.

Christians today use the same song to thank God for the way he cares for them and all the world.

You provide the earth with crops. You send rain on the ploughed fields and soak them with water; you soften the soil with showers and make young plants grow. What a rich harvest your goodness provides!

From Psalm 65 of the Bible

God provides everything people need.

4 Let's look at
Good times

Isn't it great
when everything works
out right.
When people are loving,
fair and kind.
When the world seems
full of new life,
new hope,
new joy.
When everything seems
just right,
as it should be.

The Bible says
that when God made the world
it was very good.

Here is a joyful song from
the Bible
that Christians sing to God.

Come on everyone,
sing to God,
come to him,
with your joyful songs.
He made us,
we belong to him,
he takes care of us.
God is good.
His love never changes
and it will last for ever.

From Psalm 100 of the Bible

God is good.

5 Let's look at

Bad times

We don't like to think about bad times:
about people who are unkind,
who quarrel and fight.
About how people get hurt.
About how things get broken.
About the bad things
that make the whole world
a sad place.

Christians believe that God made a good world and that he hates it when people choose to do bad things. Their wrongdoing has spoiled it all.

It has become a cruel place: there is hurting and death, and great unhappiness.

Once, God sent a flood to destroy all the evil in the world. Even so, he saved Noah, because he was a good man, along with his family and two of every kind of creature.

God takes care of those who live as he wants
but is angry with those who do wrong;
he is a good and fair judge.
From Psalm 7 of the Bible

God is always fair.

6 Let's look at
Rules

Imagine being in a forest
where there were no paths...
Trying to find your way
would be hard in daytime
but even harder at night.
But imagine that you find a path
that leads you
where you want to go.
Would you even think of going off the
path?

Rules can be like a path
that shows you where to go,
that keeps you out of trouble.
The Bible says
that when people disobeyed God
they lost their way
and didn't know how they should live.
God gave them rules,
laws,
to guide them.

Dear God,
you have given us your laws
and told us to obey them
all through our lives.
They show us the path we should
follow.
The people who stay on that path
will find real happiness,
and you will keep them safe.

From Psalm 119 of the Bible

God has given laws to guide people.

7 Let's look at
Dads

There are all kinds of
dads:
best of all is a dad
who really loves you,
who knows what is
best for you.

Jesus Christ, the person who Christians are named after, told a story about a really loving father.

There was once a young man who didn't want to live at home anymore. He took his share of the family money and went off to have a good time.

He spent all his money. Then he couldn't get a job. He didn't have any food. He thought: The people who work on Dad's farm live better than this. Why don't I go home?

He traveled back. How stupid he'd been. What a waste of the family money. What would he say? What excuse did he have?

But his dad saw him coming while he was still a long way off. He went rushing out to meet him.

He welcomed him home and threw a party!

And that, said Jesus, is how God welcomes anyone who stops doing bad things, who decides to come back to God and live as God wants.

From the book Luke wrote about Jesus in the Bible

God is a loving father.

8 Let's look at
Moms

Moms can be many things:
it's great to have a mom who
really loves you whatever you
do, who knows what to do
when you're scared,
who looks after you when
you're ill.

Long ago, a grown-up
wrote this prayer:

Dear God,
I have stopped worrying
about all the things
I cannot control.
Instead, I trust in you
to take care of me,
and I feel as safe
as a child
in its mother's arms.

From Psalm 131 of the Bible

God is like a loving mother.

9 Let's look at
Families

Think about families:
parents, brothers and sisters.
It can be good to have
them around
because they understand
what it's like
to live in your home.
They know what kind of
problems you face.
They might even help you
out.

Christians believe that
God himself
came to this world
as the baby Jesus
and grew up
in an ordinary family.
He knows what it's like
to live in this world
and how hard it can be
to do what is right.
Jesus said this:

*Whoever does what
God wants
is my brother, my sister
and my mother.*

**From the book Matthew wrote
about Jesus in the Bible**

**God is like someone in
your family who really
understands and cares.**

People who care

It's hard work looking after things.

Imagine looking after a flock of sheep.

Long ago, in Israel, a young boy called David had to look after his flock of sheep.
He had to find them food and water,
he had to protect them from danger.
When he was older he became a soldier and faced even worse dangers.
But he believed that just as he had looked after his sheep,
God was looking after him.

This is a song that David wrote:

God is my shepherd.
He gives me everything I need.
He lets me rest in fields of green grass.
He takes me to pools of clear water.
He helps me on my way.
He protects me from danger.

From Psalm 23 of the Bible

Christians believe that God takes care of them in just the same way.

God is the good shepherd.

11 Let's look at
Being rescued

Imagine getting into danger.
How glad you are
when someone comes to help
and takes you to safety
without scolding you.

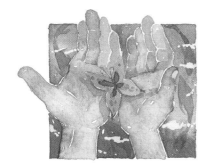

Christians believe that God loves
the people of this world.
The Bible is full of stories
of how God took care of his
people, the Israelites.
He rescued them when they were
slaves to the people in Egypt.

He brought them to a new land.
He helped them in battles against cruel enemies.
Even when they disobeyed him and were punished,
he was always ready to forgive them and help them
again. This is what they said about God:

*Our God
is a God who saves.
He rescues us from death.*
From Psalm 68 of the Bible

God is a rescuer.

Friends

Hooray for friends!
Real friends.
People who like you
just as you are.
You can talk about anything together.
You can have fun or be quiet together.
You know your friend cares about you
and will keep a promise.

Christians believe that God
made people to be his friends.
He cannot be friendly
to those who do wrong,
but he is always ready to
forgive anyone who is sorry.
Here is a prayer from the Bible
for people who want to be
friends with God:

Dear God,
You have promised to forgive
all the wrong things I have
done.
I know you will teach me how
to do right things
if I am willing to obey you.
Dear God, you are the friend
of those who obey you,
and you keep your promises.
From Psalm 25 of the Bible

God is a friend.

13 Let's look at

Air

Does air exist?
Of course it does!
Even though you cannot see air,
you know it is there.
You feel the air that you breathe
to stay alive.
You feel the air moving,
blowing your hair;
hear it rustling the leaves,
see it bending the trees,
making the ocean waves...

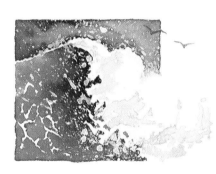

The Bible says
that God is spirit.
Invisible as the wind,
but more powerful than a storm.
Unseen as the air we breathe,
but giving people new life.

God, who is spirit,
changes us.
His spirit fills us with
power, love and self-control.

**From Paul's second letter to the Christians in
Corinth and his second letter to Timothy, in the
Bible**

**God's unseen power
can change people . . . and
the world.**

Who is God?

1   God is the maker of the world.

2   God is the giver of life.

3   God provides everything people need.

4   God is good.

5   God is always fair.

6   God has given laws to guide people.

7   God is a loving father.

8   God is like a loving mother.

9   God is like someone in your family who really understands and cares.

10 God is the good shepherd.

11 God is a rescuer.

12 God is a friend.

13 God's unseen power can change people . . . and the world.